WHAT EVERY *CC*
HIGH SCHOOL STUDENT
DOESN'T KNOW... YET

A Guide for the College-Bound

WHAT EVERY HIGH SCHOOL STUDENT DOESN'T KNOW... YET

A Guide for the College-Bound

Lucia S. Smith

rabbit's
foot
press™

A division of Blue Mountain Arts
Boulder, Colorado

Library of Congress Catalog Card Number: 2004025742
ISBN: 1-58786-015-5

Certain trademarks are used under license.

Printed in the United States of America.
First Printing: 2005

 This book is printed on recycled paper.

This book is printed on fine quality, laid embossed, 80 lb. paper. This paper has been specially produced to be acid free (neutral pH) and contains no groundwood or unbleached pulp. It conforms with all the requirements of the American National Standards Institute, Inc., so as to ensure that this book will last and be enjoyed by future generations.

Library of Congress Cataloging-in-Publication Data

Smith, Lucia S., 1982-
  What every high school student doesn't know--yet : a guide for the college-bound / Lucia S. Smith.
    p. cm.
  ISBN 1-58786-015-5 (trade paper : alk. paper) 1. College student orientation. I. Title.

  LB2343.3.S66 2004
  378.1'98--dc22

                                        2004025742
                                        CIP

Blue Mountain Arts, Inc.
P.O. Box 4549, Boulder, Colorado 80306

For B.

CONTENTS

"I Used To Be Cool... "

"Um, Are You Serious?"

Upis, Etc.

"Will This Be On The Test?"

Some Stuff for the Folks at Home

"I USED TO BE COOL..."
Making the Transition to College

So you were prom king. So you didn't even go to prom. So you starred in every school musical. So you did forty hours of community service every week. So you had an after-school job. So you graduated at the top of your class. So you graduated at the bottom of your class.

So what?

High school is the best of times, it is the worst of times, but as you head off to college, what is most important to remember is that it is the *past* of times. Some people had terrific times in high school, making lifelong friends and doing well both academically and personally. Others hated high school and remember it as a series of pointless activities with intolerable and intolerant people. In either case, making the transition to college is, at the very least, the beginning of something new.

But we'll get to that in a minute. First, let me tell you to enjoy and make the most of the summer before you enter college. Go on a trip with your best friend. Get a job and save up your money. Hide in your room reading every book your school banned and playing every video game your parents wouldn't let you play until you finished your homework. Hey, watch old reruns of *The Price is Right* every day, if that's your thing. No matter what, make sure you spend plenty of time with your hometown friends, because this won't be possible once you head off to college. As for your parents, they're probably footing at least part of the bill for college, but even if they aren't, I'm willing to bet they are partly responsible for the things that make your life good (or at least tolerable), so make sure you thank them at least once. And don't be surprised if they act like jerks during the summer. Their lives are changing too, and they're probably a little sad, happy, and confused. They've known you all your life, and they'll miss you, whether you (or they) believe it or not, even if you're only going across town.

Unless you somehow grew up on a college campus, the first time you set foot in your new dorm room or sit down in your first class you will feel out of your element. It's fine to think, "Hey, this is just high school but with a big campus and without bells between classes" — but this thought isn't going to get you anywhere. Your high school may have prepared you well academically for college and you may have been a straight-A student, but the bottom line is this is a new place with new people and new expectations. **It's okay to be scared. Hey, it's okay to be petrified.** This is not to say I think you should run around asking everyone to hold you or call your parents every five minutes. Just be aware that confusion is normal and that in a few weeks you'll be laughing at how bewildered you used to be.

Even if you swear that you're not scared of college and this new school will be a breeze, it's extremely important to remember that **while you may be the same person, you're now surrounded by new people**. You may be going to school in your hometown, or even commuting from your old home, but you will still be starting off among strangers. Who are these people? I can pretty much guarantee that at your new school there will be people smarter than you, dumber than you, people who play the piano better than you, and people who are worse at singing. Once college begins, though, everyone is on the same playing field.

Continuing that thought, **you are just as smart (and dumb) as everyone else**. It's common to lose all confidence when entering college. You see other kids who seem to have tons of friends immediately, never ask professors questions, and breeze through tests. You may have a different style, you may be a different kind of learner, and you may read questions more thoroughly. Whatever the differences, you are just as ready to do as well as the students that surround you. Getting into college is a two-way system. Your school may look like it's bricks and mortar, but you two are in a relationship. Just as you want to do well in school and get a good job, your school wants you to go on to do great things. It needs you to be an example of its quality, and it wouldn't accept you if it didn't think you would be smart enough and have the skills to survive. So fear not; you are about to learn what every high school student doesn't know about college... yet.

"UM, ARE YOU SERIOUS?"

Dealing with Yourself and Others
Freshman Year

I'm a Little Messy. . .

Depending on when you're reading this, you may have received the names and addresses of your future roommate(s) or may be waiting for the list to arrive. **If you already have the name of your roommate(s), write to him or her (or them)... now. If you're waiting for the name, write to him or her... as soon as you can after you receive it.**

Writing to the person who will share your teeny, tiny living space for the next year is important and fun. First, it's the best possible way to ensure that you don't overpack, bringing the same things as the other person. When it comes to appliances and electronics, it makes sense to coordinate, especially if you have two or more roommates. Asking who is bringing what is a great excuse for getting in touch before school without seeming like that uncool person who is a little too excited for the school year to start. **There is really no need for five large lamps and two refrigerators in a double room.**

Writing also helps break the ice. **There's no need to start living with a new person without any information about him or her**. Ask what kind of activities he or she did in high school, what he or she does after school, what major he or she is thinking about. The more you know, the easier it will be to talk about things in those awkward first days.

If nothing else, it's also hilarious to look back on your letters to each other and the impressions they gave. I've had friends who have thought their roommates were going to be the exact opposite of how they actually were. It's hard to describe yourself in a letter. Believe me, you'll be entertained at the end of the year thinking about how you thought the year would turn out. Even if the letter is accurate, people change, and you can laugh about how the roommate who promised he would be a famous actor by the end of college quickly became a bio major thanks to a great lab course. If you don't want to write, pick up the phone and call. However you do it, get in touch.

Rentals Make the World Go Round

Let's look ahead to your college summers for a minute. Look, I know you're attached to your stuff. I know that your TV is perfect in every way and that the VCR obeys your every command. But I also know this: **carrying things across the country is possibly the worst experience you'll have in college.** As someone who has flown or driven to and from school many times and begged more friends than I can count to take my stuff for the summer, let me preach to you the beauty of rentals.

Most schools rent refrigerators, microwaves, televisions, and other bulky stuff. **These rentals can sometimes be pricey, but they usually come in package deals.** You can split the cost with your roommate(s), and it could very well still be less than paying for that overweight box on an airplane. Besides, all appliances you rent from school meet dorm regulations and you don't have to worry about hurting your precious television in transit.

If you're lucky, you'll have a whole load of friends who live within driving distance of school and are willing to hold your things for the summer. Still, you probably have a lot of large things (can you say "bookshelf"?) that you need to store on or around campus. Most schools offer storage deals, but they are often inconvenient, expensive, or both. **If you have just one friend with a car, beg that person, offer treats, money, whatever, and rent a storage space at an independent company in town.** I shared a storage unit with three other people my sophomore year and it only cost me about thirty dollars for the entire summer. It takes a little extra effort, but rentals and storage lockers can save your sanity.

Finally, before you carry everything you think you can't rent to college, remember that you're not moving into the wilderness. Guess what — school stores carry school supplies. They know you're coming, and they know what you need. Don't waste space (unless you have a lot) carrying easily-replaceable, fairly cheap items to school. What you can't rent, buy, and what you can't buy, you probably didn't need anyway.

Reinventing Yourself

College is a new beginning. No more parents, no more siblings, no more rules. Okay, that last one's a myth. **Unless your entire graduating class is following you to school, your new classmates and friends aren't going to know much about you.** They won't know you cry at scary movies, that your hamster is your best friend, or that you just got out of a semi-tragic, five-year relationship. It's easy to consider college a golden opportunity to start over; to go back and reinvent yourself into the person you always wanted to be.

My biggest piece of advice here is to **be careful.** Don't get lost in trying to create an image that isn't really you. If you don't want to share the fact that your brother has a third arm or that you were a huge geek in high school, no worries. There's no reason to tell people things that aren't their business. I've seen many situations, usually with freshmen, where people assume that telling secrets or strange stories will gain them friends. It's understandable to want to be the center of attention your first week of college, to want everyone to be interested in you and who you are, but don't get carried away. Telling exaggerated stories about yourself gets you brief attention, not long-lasting friends. I guarantee that bragging about that wild prom hot-tub party adventure will do nothing but turn you into "that kid who did all that stuff at prom." **College is a fresh start, but don't forget who you really are.**

"My freshman year I met a girl named Babs. She claimed that people had always called her Babs and she didn't know where the name came from. A few weeks later I met a girl who went to high school with Babs. She told me that no one had called her Babs in high school and that she had made the story up completely to sound cool. The whole thing seemed strange to me, and I stopped hanging out with Babs. I didn't think I could really trust her."

— Julie, St. John's

Top Five...
Reasons Not To Pack A Lot
Of Clothes

* Nobody wears anything but jeans and hoodies.
* Nobody wears anything but shorts and T-shirts.
* Nobody wears anything but sweats.
* Nobody wears anything they didn't get for free at school.
* Did you see the size of that closet you're sharing?

Meeting New People

Meeting new people is one of the most fun and funny experiences of college. From the first day you enter your new dorm room to the day you put on your graduation cap, you'll be meeting new people and finding out things you never knew about your college friends. Freshman year, my RA (resident advisor) held a group activity in which she invited a representative from the Lesbian/Gay Alliance to come speak to us. The first question the representative asked was, "Do you feel this school is more liberal than where you came from?" I was shocked to see almost all hands around me go up. I come from an extremely diverse area — racially, economically, and religiously. For the first time in my life, I was surrounded by a majority of people who had never met people with a lot less money than they have, people of different races, or even people from outside their home state. One girl told me she had never met a person who wasn't Christian, another guy told me he had never left California.

Just as it's important to realize that everyone around you belongs in school with you, it's incredibly important to be prepared for differences, and not to dismiss people just because they aren't like you. While I found it strange to meet people whose worlds had been more homogeneous than mine, there were people at the meeting who found me strange for not believing in what they had always believed to be right. I know it sounds corny, but as we got to know each other, I became great friends with the people in my RA group despite the fact that we had different life experiences and held different views of the world. Hey, often that's what spiced up our conversations. My closest friends freshman year were a girl who claimed that the movie *Varsity Blues* was based on her high school, a star student from the Dominican Republic, and a conservative guy from a political family. I am similar to none of these people, but we had a great time together. The people you will meet during college will come from backgrounds very different from your own. You're not in college to meet your twin.

Ahhhh, Roommates

The golden rule of meeting new people is *keep an open mind,* and this can be applied to dealing with your roommates. Freshman year a friend of mine had eight roommates. They all got along well, and six of them even lived together again sophomore year. This is not to say, however, that these were eight similar people.

My friend claims the only reason they all were able to live together peaceably was tolerance.

When one of her roommates started spraying the phone with disinfectant once a week, they all just laughed and let her do it. When another brought her boyfriend into their communal shower, they told her not to do it again, but laughed about it. **Simply having an open mind will take you far in college, let alone life.** Obviously, your roommates aren't going to be perfect. Even your best friends annoy you once in a while, and everything becomes magnified when you are sharing a room with another person. Just remember that your best friends were once strangers and that you have plenty of quirks yourself, and you'll be fine.

That said, don't be a pushover. If your roommates are mooching off you, are mean to you, are irrational or depressed, don't just look the other way. I've had friends with roommates who had extreme mood swings, were compulsive liars, and one who went off medication and "jokingly" attacked her. If you ever feel in personal danger, tell someone who can help you: an adviser, a person in the housing office, a professor. If you find yourself in an extreme situation, it may be possible to change rooms or have a room meeting with a mediator (and this works more often than you would believe). Overall, try to remember that this is a new situation for everyone, and most people aren't used to sharing space with a stranger. Give suggestions, not orders. Treat others with the same respect that you would like from them. Whether you have one roommate or share a suite with ten other people, whether you are good friends or not, your first roommates will be the ones you always remember. **Always, always be willing to laugh.**

Top Five...
Theme Parties

* Toga! Toga! Toga!
* South of the Border
* Jungle Fever
* Eighth Grade Dance Party
* Wild, Wild West

Living in a Dorm

Dorm life is in no way ideal. The rooms are small, you share a bathroom with multiple people you don't really know, and chances are at least once you're going to stand outside picking at the carpet for three hours waiting for campus security to come let you into your room after you lose your key. (Or was that just me?) By the time you finish your freshman year, you will be very appreciative of your home, mostly because you miss all the space and privacy you never even realized you had, even if you shared a room with your younger sister. But dorm life can also rule. I know you're sitting there thinking, "Is she going to tell me how getting strange foot diseases from a clogged communal shower forty feet away down a dingy hall is fun?" Well, sure.

Okay, maybe I just lied. I grant there is nothing pleasant about dirty bathrooms or cramped spaces, but as you'll find again and again, **it's all about attitude**, and there are a few things you can do to make your life a little bit easier. First, remember how easy you have it. Someone picks up the garbage for you, someone is in charge of your electricity, someone will come and exterminate should you have a bug problem. Most importantly, *no one is in charge of you.* You're freeeee (but check the dorm rules, or expect fines at the end of the year).

The second rule is to pack lightly. I say this calmly, but it's extremely important. I know that every pair of shoes is cute and that every white t-shirt is essential, but remember that you have to carry what you decide to bring and fit it into a small space, and that you can and will undoubtedly buy more when you get there. You're not moving into the middle of nowhere; forget the shampoo and conditioner and leave the pair of shoes you've only worn once and the sixth pair of khaki pants. You'll be happier later, especially when you don't have to bring clothes home because you know that you already have things there.

Third, **be clean**. Don't worry, I don't mean pick up all your clothes and make your bed every day. I fully subscribe to the messy bed method of life, but that does not mean you should let chaos rule. When it comes to living with someone, I suggest you follow the rule that my roommates and I have always followed: no matter what happens, no matter how many papers you need to spread out, how many pants you need to try on, how many books you need to have, **always keep the center of your floor clean**. As long as the center of the room is clean, the neat people are happy because they can at least walk across the room and the messy people are happy because their things can go anywhere else.

On to the fourth rule of better dorm living: **don't stomp on the floor or bang on the walls**. As someone who used to live below some jerks who literally *hammered* the floor, I can't stress this enough. Dorm walls and ceilings are thin, and it is nothing but annoying to have the people above you jumping around or constantly moving things. Of course you can move around, have parties, whatever — just be aware that you aren't alone. Don't make unnecessary noise unless you're willing to take the same from the people above you. If you live on the top floor, that's another story...

The next rule to surviving a dorm is **don't be stupid — be careful, be aware, and think**. Maybe it's not smart to try flushing an already overfull toilet in order to clear it. Maybe it's a bad sign that the shower has slimy green stuff in it. Maybe you shouldn't invite fifty of your closest friends over to party in your hallway. The laws of physics and annoyed neighbors say you will flood the bathroom, get a foot fungus, and find yourself facing the wrath of your entire entryway. So unless you want to be explaining how sorry you are about going to the bathroom in the sink (true story, unfortunately — and no, not about me!), think before you do something.

Finally, this is the most important rule of all to enjoying college life: **be nicer to the janitors than you have ever been to anyone in your entire life**. These people are both hardworking and in complete control of your life, so why not be nice? Believe me, you're going to be happy you said that extra hello or asked how his or her day was when your light bulbs burn out and you need more toilet paper. Plus, they deserve thanks just for keeping any kind of order in a place full of people like you.

Dealing with Parents

Perhaps the most important thing you should know about arriving at college is how to deal with what isn't there: your parents. I could say that parents are great, that parents are annoying, blah, blah, blah. I don't know your family, so I'll just leave it at the fact that in most cases, although they're not actually with you at school, your parents are going to be forces in your life, even if you've flown 3,000 miles away from them.

Once they've let you go, parents can exert any number of pressures on you, especially during your freshman year — the most popular being expressed as, "We're not paying for you to get bad grades." After years of hearing people's parents say this, I can only come to the conclusion that they aren't thinking things out. If only you had *known* they weren't paying for you to get bad grades, you wouldn't have tried so hard to be humiliated by that Spanish quiz — right? Your parents might also complain that you never call home or might call you constantly.

While these things aren't necessarily related, I can give you the same advice for them — **don't worry, be happy (and study).** You know that your parents (and you) want you to do well, so study. If you try your hardest and don't do well, you should let them know (nicely) that their constant demands aren't helping. **If you don't even try, you deserve to get yelled at**. As for not calling home, college is a crazy, busy time and parents somehow forget this between their college years and yours. So make a date with your parents to talk every other Sunday. That way your parents know you'll eventually call, and you don't have to worry. Also, if your parents have a computer, a little "Hi, I'm alive," e-mail never hurt anyone.

There is one more major issue with parents that arises once you go off to college: your freedom. Being in a new place with just your friends and no real limitations, it's easy to think you'll have the same freedom when you return home for vacation. Not so. The only answer is to compromise. Your parents made you and they will yell at you. Just explain why they can trust you and hope for a middle ground. If all else fails, stomp on the ground and yell — works every time.

Dealing with Yourself

College *rules.* It rules because probably for the first time in your life you are on your own. You can get up when you want, choose when to go to classes, eat whatever, and go out whenever. The other side of this is that you are also on your own to deal with the stress and various challenges that will come your way. I'm sure that your RA will cover all this, but in case you need someone else to tell you, let me say it: **talk to people when you are having problems.**

I don't care if it's your dad or the lady who works in the dining hall, just make sure that you are taking care of yourself. Most colleges have an amazing variety of resources for people who are having emotional, mental, or physical problems. At most schools the first few (and sometimes as many as a dozen) counseling sessions at the health center are free, and always confidential. So, if you have a problem or just something that is upsetting you, there's no reason not to take advantage of all the counselors and people trained to help you.

There is help out there for you, even if your problem is just that you are worried about a friend. Colleges are well equipped, so don't use the "no one will understand" excuse. If you're worried about someone else, **there are plenty of support groups.** Just contact your health center and ask. There is no need to feel self-conscious or embarrassed; these groups wouldn't exist if there weren't a demand for them. Group sessions can sometimes be the most helpful.

"My sophomore year I was feeling overwhelmed with work. I tried to talk to my advisor, but he wasn't much help. I then talked to a counselor. He helped me a lot, giving me advice on how to deal with stress. I totally recommend going to talk to different people. Don't give up if the first person you ask isn't right for you. There's always someone who understands."

— Tom, Emory University

Top Five...
Ways to Ask Your Parents
for Money

* You're investing in my future.
* If I get a job, that'll take away from study time.
* I need money for food. You don't want me to starve, do you?
* It's because of all the long-distance calls to you!
* Puhleeeeeeeeeeze!

The Big School/Small School Syndrome

I went to a large high school, with a graduating class of just under eight hundred. My senior-year gym class had forty-six students in it. That's one more than there was in my freshman roommate's entire graduating class. The moral of this story? **When getting ready for college, get ready for the number of people going with you**. It can be quite a shock to go from a small private or public school to a 40,000-person state university, or from a really big school to a small college. Just as some of my roommates have sometimes felt lost among 5,000 other students, old high school friends of mine sometimes feel cramped in 1,000-person colleges.

If you're going to a school much larger than the one you left, try to learn as much about it as you can. While most schools promise a warm and fuzzy feeling when you enter, it's unlikely that you'll find the kind of personal attention you may have had in high school. The more you know about a school, its departments, teachers, and activities, the easier your adjustment will be. If you seek out people, they will respond to you, but you can't arrive and expect teachers, classes, and activities to come to you. Knowing what you're dealing with helps you have a realistic idea of what to expect as you enter your freshman year, and also helps you take advantage of it all.

If you're going to a school much smaller than your high school, try to learn as much about it as you can. Seems kind of strange that I would use this advice twice, but if you're worried that you are going to feel limited, try to find out all the activities your new school has to offer. I'm sure you'll find that even the smallest schools have dozens of clubs. If there's something you think is missing, start your own club, and if you're worried about seeing too much of the same people, try to find an off-campus activity. If you are truly in the middle of nowhere, I suggest you buy some running shoes and take up exercise as a way to get away from feeling confined.

Joining Activities

I don't know you. I don't know what clothes you wear, what movies you like, or what you did in high school. What I do know is this: there is a club or activity for you at your future school. How do I know this, having never met you? I know because **there is an extra-curricular activity for everyone. Yes, everyone**. And while there is the unlikely chance that you won't find a club you want to join, it is one hundred percent possible to start your own group.

Before you join thirteen groups, let me introduce you to one of the many strange differences between high school and college. In high school you can take eight classes a day, work an after-school job, be on the track team, and edit the yearbook. You can write plays, be captain of the speech team, run the film club, and still have time to hang out and do your homework. In college you take four or five classes a few times a week. So, you should be able to do even more activities, right? *Wrong*. **For reasons beyond anyone's comprehension, just existing in college will take up way more time than it did in high school**. If you try to join five different groups, tutor, and take four classes, something will have to give. Unless you are the most focused person on earth and are willing to sacrifice a social life, it's just not possible to do as many different things as you did in high school. Don't ask me why, just believe me and let's move on.

College is more than work and it's much more than partying. It's a perfect time to find out all the things you're really good at or really interested in or, even better, both. Ever wondered if you could be an actor, a teacher, or work in a foreign country? Audition. Tutor. Volunteer as a translator at a school or hospital with an immigrant population. **Freshman year is the best time to get involved** so don't let the opportunity pass you by. Requirements and job hunting will come soon — find something you're passionate about now so you don't have excuses later for not doing it.

Getting a J-O-B

There are two ways to think about getting a job in college, even for those who have to work in order to pay for their education. There's the "These four years are for school — I have the rest of my life to work" philosophy, and then there's the "Show me the money" attitude. Both are completely valid.

Unless you are incredibly rich or lazy, you will no doubt spend a good deal of your life working, and unless you go for degree after degree, it's true that you will never have the opportunity to explore and enjoy a university environment again. Having a job while in school can take up a lot of time and energy that could be spent doing things like playing (or watching) sports, throwing parties, pursuing original research, becoming a painter, practicing the cello, or just hanging out. **Before you start filling out W-4 forms, take a minute to consider whether you'd rather be working in the library on Friday nights or going to a campus event with your friends.**

That said, there are three great reasons to get a job while in college.

1: **Jobs now = jobs later**. Having experience in the workforce, any sort of experience, shows future bosses you have initiative, organization, and some knowledge of what it means to put in the hours on a regular basis. Most jobs in college are part-time but can still give you lots of responsibility without much worry. Plus, you may work for someone who can give you a job during the summer or after graduation, or can help you make contacts.

2: Maybe you're actually interested in what you're doing! **Having a job doesn't have to mean working long hours in the dining hall** (though some people think that's a lot of fun). Besides the more "functional" jobs, you could be a research assistant to a professor or work at a school-related job, like being a Resident Advisor, a position which does not pay directly, but usually assures you free housing. These jobs are great ways to learn if you really enjoy a certain subject or working with other people. If you're interested in journalism, layout, or selling ads, get involved with the campus newspaper.

Finally, there's the most popular reason of all to work.

3: **The money**. College costs a lot, and (excuse the rhyme) most people need to earn while they learn. Tons of students are on financial aid, and they are sought after for university jobs that sometimes pay quite well. Even if you don't have to, working just five hours a week can help a lot. Five hours isn't much time (who among us hasn't killed five hours on a *Real World* marathon?), but the extra forty or fifty dollars a week can really affect the number of things you are able to do while at school.

Many students are torn between needing or wanting extra cash and not wanting to sacrifice their grades. If you want to earn money without losing too much time for classes, I advise you to work at a circulation desk in your school's library. Unlike other kinds of work, library jobs are often active only in spurts. It's usually completely fine to bring your own books and essentially get paid to do your homework.

Working during college can be annoying. It takes up time that you could be spending on other things. It's often the case that it's a financial necessity. If work is a major part of your college experience, your undergraduate life will be different, but — guess what? — you'll still get that degree, and you'll learn a little something about the working world while you're at it.

The Dining Hall vs. You

No one wants to go to college and gain the dreaded "freshman fifteen." These are the pounds you find yourself putting on when you are allowed to pick your own food and are suddenly surrounded by people who love pizza and cola (and beer) as much as you do. For the first time, you're free to eat ice cream four times a day, mashed potatoes for every meal, or simply drink a lot. Believe me, it's great, but it's also an easy way to gain unexpected and unwelcome pounds.

Now that I've warned you, I'll tell you this: **the thing you need to remember when entering college is not to worry too much about what you eat**. Just as it's simple to overeat, it's also easy to overanalyze your eating and stop yourself from getting the nutrients you need or even simply deprive yourself of the joy of eating. **If you're really concerned about your eating habits, plan ahead.** Take a look at your college's dining halls and their options. If you know you like variety, try to eat a little of each food group at every dinner. If you know you like one type of food, spice things up and build around that certain dish. For example, if you know you love bagels, make bagel pizzas or turkey sandwiches on bagels. Hey, use a bagel to hold your salad. That way, you get to eat your favorite food and make it nutritious. And you never know how good salad dressing is on bread until you try.

When it comes to dining hall eating, creativity is a means of survival. Make root beer floats, add grilled chicken to your salads, heat up your shredded cheese and make nachos. Whatever you can think up, you should try. Ask around — you'll be surprised by how creative people can be. One other thing to do to avoid gaining weight is to drink healthy. Just as you need to have balanced meals, don't drink soda or heavily sweetened fruit drinks at every meal. Try to drink one glass of water before you have anything else. That way, if you're not really thirsty, you avoid unnecessary sugar. Drinking milk is a great way to get your calcium for great teeth.

Student's Best Friend

No, I'm not talking about dogs (though I hear they are very nice). I'm talking about your computer. Assuming you're lucky enough to be able to buy one, college might be the first time you'll have a computer all to yourself, and it's important to pick the right one. I can't even pretend to know enough about different models of computers to give you advice, but I can talk about the size of your computer.

Desktops are large and sit on your desk, laptops are small and can be easily moved. Both have their advantages and disadvantages. Desktops are harder to pack, harder to carry, harder to store. Once you install one, it doesn't leave your desk. They also have larger monitors, are generally faster, and have more memory than laptops. With laptops, you pay for their compactness. You lose some features in exchange for portability, and you also run a greater risk of damage to or theft of the computer itself. Some people swear by their desktops, others by their laptops.

If you always work in your room, get a desktop. It'll probably last longer and be able to store more information. If you're like me, however — always moving — a laptop is definitely a better choice. They are extremely convenient, and most libraries and student centers now have Ethernet plugs or wireless connections so you can hook up to the Internet outside your room.

No matter what, remember to save your work and back up your files. Computers crash, sprinklers go off, buildings get locked, theft happens. Do this with every new file, and your best friend will never turn around and bite you.

Top Five...
Ways to Become Unpopular
Really Quickly

* Telling everyone to be quiet after 10 PM.
* Always showing up dressed perfectly for a 9 AM class.
* Plastering your room with pictures of yourself.
* Wearing your roommates' clothes without asking.
* Always being "that guy."

Money, Money, Money

Money can be the most difficult subject to tackle in college. I'd love to tell you that it's usually a problem that students have too much money, but that would be a big, fat lie. But while all of us could use, or at least would like to have, more money, the main problem is how to handle what little money we have.

Even before you arrive on campus (and constantly after) companies will offer you credit cards. Don't get sucked into believing that because you don't have to pay the bills immediately, you don't have to pay eventually. Every year, countless college students go into debt because they don't understand how to be smart about their money. Don't let yourself fall into this trap; it takes years to dig yourself out of debt, and a bad credit record can follow you for the rest of your life. Money you get from your parents is also absolutely real — they probably worked hard to get it, and it is not endless, unless your parents happen to run the Department of the Treasury.

Budget. Decide (A) what you need and (B) what you want; at the very least try to buy more from Column A than Column B.

Don't wait for that first whopping late penalty or bounced check fee to learn the merits of paying bills and balancing accounts. Beyond understanding the basics of credit cards and checks, there are plenty of ways to save money if you're on a tight budget. Here are a few key ways to save money, now in convenient list form! (I grant that this is the only form in which this information has ever been.)

* If you can't afford a computer or a printer, **use a campus computer lab**. Computer use is free in labs and printing can often be very cheap. **Sometimes you can even use paper from the printer lab for your own printer** — just make sure there is enough for other people and that you aren't breaking a campus rule.

* Textbooks can be your biggest expense in college, costing several hundred dollars per semester. **Buy used books or ask friends who have taken the same class if you can use, buy, or even have their books**. In any case, think hard about which books you really need to own. Most colleges and universities ask that all professors put their required books on reserve at the university library; if your school doesn't have this policy, try to get it started. Bottom line: **it is always free to use the library.**

* **Look for free food. Gather food from dining halls and campus events**. This does not mean you should steal trays and trays of food. On your way out, just take a few extra pieces of fruit, or grab some cereal in a plastic cup. Little trips to the convenience store late at night add up quickly — by planning ahead you can save quite a bit of money. **Also, go to every single meeting or study break you can**. There will *always* **be free food at Resident Advisor-sponsored study breaks.** Take advantage and go grab those pretzels, cookies, and cans of soda. Go to the Hanukkah potato pancake party at the Hillel, enjoy egg roll night at the Asian Students Association, or tapas at Spanish cultural night. It's a great way to meet new people as well as get a free meal. College savings can boil down to stockpiling and creative grazing.

* **Look for cheap entertainment.** It's easy not to think about how expensive things will become as you set out for dinner or a night of bar hopping or clubbing. Costs can add up fast. Even if your date is treating, chances are you'll be paying for something, and even if you set out planning not to eat or drink at all, just water can cost upwards of five dollars in a trendy place. Look for alternatives like campus plays, room parties, or other events that will cost either nothing or under ten dollars total. It's fine to go out clubbing, but if you make it a four-nights-a-week

habit you'll find yourself out of cash extremely quickly. Believe me, you can have just as much fun at a dance party with friends in your room as out on the town.

* **Be a bad host.** If you're truly short on money and still want to have a social life, volunteer your room for parties, but promise the room and nothing more. You can be in charge of setting up, but other people are in charge of supplying food and drinks. This way people have a place to party, and you don't have to pay for it. If people think this is unfair, volunteer to help them clean up their next party as compensation. There are plenty of creative ways to make up for not being able to pay.

* **Finally, try to make vacations cheap.** By the time you get to your spring break, you may be looking to go away with your friends rather than going home. In this case, try to do things that are close by. If you go to school near a city, stay on campus during break, but go into the city every day and walk around. Take time to see the sights, a baseball game, whatever you don't have time to do during the school year. **If you do want to go away, I suggest driving with friends rather than flying, and going to a place where you know someone to stay with**. Road trips are hilarious and fun, and if everyone is happy and willing, the journey can be more fun than your actual destination. Just bring a camera, some CDs, and let the good times roll.

UPIS, ETC.

Unidentifed Party Injuries and Other Hazards of a College Social Life

Freshman Orientation

Freshman orientation is likely the first real encounter you will have with your new school. Don't dread it, and above all, don't skip it. It's extremely important because it influences how you perceive your school and how others at the school will perceive you. **As they say, there's never a second chance to make a first impression**. Orientation can be separated into three categories: the Good, the Bad, and the Ugly.

Let's start with the Good. **Orientation can be great**. Meetings and programs give you a chance to meet new people. If you are shy, orientation events force you to talk to others, ask about their backgrounds and opinions, and talk about yourself. If you're social, here's a chance to start assembling your new set of friends. **Colleges want you to be excited about school and the next four years, so their opening events are often a lot of fun.** They bring in cool speakers, put on pretty funny sketches, and usually end (or start) with free food.

Orientation isn't all fun and games, so onto the Bad. **The worst thing about orientation events is that they often go on too long.** Once they herd everyone into a room, people start talking, the room temperature rises, and it seems like the Dean of Whatever may never finish saying that you are the future. Depending on where you're from and what experiences you've had, many of the events may not interest you. Universities deal with a ton of people every year, and they have to address the broadest range of issues they can to accommodate the girl from a small town in California as well as the boy from Tokyo. **Be patient, try to stay awake, and keep your ears open — the best advice usually comes as a surprise**.

Finally, the Ugly. Well, there's nothing truly ugly about Orientation. **You can have a good attitude or you can have a bad attitude — it's up to you. But you should know this; both get you to the same place, into the chairs of event after event**. The only ugly thing is missing information you need. So have a good attitude and, at the very least, enjoy the free cookies.

Reputations

Who cares what people think about you? No one should be worrying about anyone else. Well, that's a great attitude, but as we all learned in high school, it's unrealistic. In reality, people notice you and will talk about you from the second you start college until the day you leave (and probably long after). Worrying about your reputation freshman year is both the silliest and the most important thing you can do.

If you're a guy and you're reading this, right now you're probably kicking up your feet and thinking, "Well, I can skip this section, only women gossip." *You wish.*

It's a common stereotype to think that only women need to worry about watching their reputations and that men don't talk about other people, especially other men. I'm here to tell you that men are as gossipy as women. They may gossip about different things, but it's still your good name on the line. I've seen men being up in each other's business more than any girl would dare to go. Seriously, guys: watch out.

So now that we know that it's natural for people to talk about each other, I'll put my advice simply: **watch what you say, and watch what you do**. This applies not just to sexual things, but everything. Don't tell anyone something you wouldn't want other people knowing. Don't do anything that you would be ashamed to tell other people. I know you'll do plenty of things you won't tell your parents, but if you're in a situation and you think at any point that you wouldn't want to tell your best friend about it, walk away. Fast. And don't put it in an e-mail later. E-mail can be, and often is, forwarded at the speed of light. Never ever describe your date last night in terms anyone might ever be tempted to circulate.

Also, **watch how you treat people**. Any time you meet a person, you make an impression. With so many new people to meet, you'll find yourself liking or disliking people based on one random encounter with them, and people will be doing the same to you. Unless you want to spend four years faking who you are, be real from day one and let life take you where it will.

Top Five...
Ways to Decorate Your Room for Cheap

* Attach butcher paper to the walls and let your friends write on it.
* Collages, collages, collages.
* Have a roommate with good taste and a lot of money.
* Hang up old record covers or posters.
* Nothing beats the simple beauty of the old "blank wall" plan.

Party, Party, Party

So are you ready to paaaaaaarty? If you're like most young adults, I'm thinking yes. Partying is a key part of college, and even if drinking, dancing, or staying up late is not your style, there are plenty of ways to have fun.

I'll start with what is, at many schools, the most popular form of entertainment, **the Greek system**. Though you probably already know this, there are two groups in the Greek system. Sororities and fraternities (for women and men, respectively, though some are coed), are the backbone of the social scene at many universities, especially the larger schools.

Sororities: Many women love sororities, but, believe it or not, sorority life can be hard. The series of parties in which you basically interview the different sororities, trying to find out which one you might like to join, is called "rush" — which gives you some idea of how little time you have to make big decisions like where you're going to live and with whom. Once that rush is over, you begin the pledge process. **During the months-long pledging process, you play bonding games, have small parties, and learn as much about your pledge house as possible**. Part of joining a sorority is proving that you care — you'll probably be asked to learn the history of your pledge house, its founders, all about other members, even the Greek alphabet.

While the pledge process can be at times annoying, boring, silly, or just plain awful, the girls who make it to the end usually think the process was worth it. After spending so much time together, you are guaranteed to make a least one new close friend. It can be a great way to meet new people if you are shy or go to a large school where it is difficult to make friends. While at some schools sorority houses force you to live together with a lot of people and learn more than you ever wanted to know about them, at other places joining a sorority can get you into nicer housing than is otherwise available. **Even if you end up hating sorority culture, you can easily find individuals in the system that you like and have bonded with**. Each sorority on a campus has its own character and attracts certain kinds of people. In all likelihood, your pledge class will be filled with people like you, so you're very likely to get along, though it may keep you from meeting people considerably different from you.

Once you've joined a sorority, the social scene can either be great or mundane, depending on what type of going-out style you have. If you enjoy large parties, beer, and meeting new people, sororities might be perfect for you. **If you enjoy a chill evening with your friends, or even going out on the town rather than going to room parties, you should make sure your sorority welcomes homebodies.** During freshman year, your sorority social life can consist mostly of parties with fraternities. I won't lie to you — frat parties can be disgusting. They are often held at filthy fraternity houses and are characterized by warm beer, loud music, and tons of drunk people. The music is usually club music, so if you enjoy dancing, or just getting lost in a crowd, it is still entirely possible to have a good time, especially if you go in with the attitude that you could possibly have fun.

Besides these parties, sorority social life is comprised of date or theme parties. **Date parties are usually held at nearby bars or in hotels and the dress code can range from nice to prom-level. Occasionally there are "shotgun" date parties, in which you have a limited amount of time (24 to 48 hours) to find a date.** There are also other theme parties where you dress up or everyone is set up by someone else. These parties can be a lot of fun, as long as you ignore the headache of trying to get things together at the last minute, or always trying to find a date. **I recommend going with your girlfriends to at least one of these parties. There's no pressure to entertain someone else and you can relax and have fun.**

Sororities also have many internal events, such as charity sales, volunteer work, or dance-a-thons.

"My pledge term had the feeling of one of those bad Monday night movies: yelling, saying that I wasn't dedicated to the house enough, and that I didn't respect the house. But in the end, this is what bonds your pledge class, this hatred of your pledge-master, and the fact that you probably have something in common after three months together."

— Elizabeth, University of Michigan

These events differ from sorority to sorority, but it is often part of your pledge to your sorority that you will give back to the community. **While they are primarily social, sororities can be a great home for the right type of person, but before you put yourself through the process, think about who you are and whether you would actually enjoy belonging to one**.

You say you're not interested in formal dances or making conversation at a get-acquainted party? Okay, I guess you're a guy. Fear not, it's on to…
Fraternities.

Fraternities can be a great choice for an incoming freshman. Most important (to some), they provide an automatic family. If you endure the pledging process and are chosen to be a member, the other guys in your frat house will be your new crowd. They will, in fact, be your brothers. You'll have people to eat with, hang out with, party with, and, on many campuses, live with. It's a great way to meet a lot of people you might ordinarily miss. Frats can also instill school pride, as you participate in sporting events and tailgate before football games.

The key difference between sororities and fraternities is that fraternities are more laid back than sororities. There is usually a period when you can go around to parties held by different fraternities and talk to the members. Once you have chosen where you want to join (and the fraternity members have chosen you), the pledging stage begins, when you go through the process of proving yourself worthy of formal initiation into the fraternity. **For fraternities, pledging involves several months of activities, though often not as formal, and sometimes much grosser, than sororities' events.** This does not mean that you won't also need to spend lots of time memorizing the history of your pledge house and its members, but getting-to-know-you events often revolve around hanging out or sports. You aren't required to play, but it's a good idea, because it's a way to get to know the other guys and get them to know and remember you.

Just as with sororities, however, there is the problem of sameness in frats. **Fraternities often look for a certain type of person, someone like them.** If you're coming to college to branch out and explore new things, try to join a frat with guys you wouldn't normally cross paths with, or avoid one altogether, so you can pick and choose your friends individually.

One last, very important caveat. **Though schools will deny it, hazing still does exist**. You may be asked to do things that range from stupid and fun to dangerous and illegal. Go with your gut. **No group is worth getting kicked out of school for and it certainly is not worth losing your life**. It will be hard at the time, but if you think you're about to do something you might regret, walk away. There are plenty of other extracurricular groups and friends to meet.

Once you join a fraternity, there are plenty of social and volunteer opportunities. **Most frats organize special volunteer events, like basketball tournaments or date auctions.** Besides these events, there is usually a volunteer coordinator. Then, of course, there are the parties. Frats usually throw the parties that sororities attend, and there are many theme parties throughout the year for fraternities and sororities. These parties range from casual to black-tie. Some parties themselves even serve as fundraisers.

Before I finish, it's important to say this: **ideally, invitations to join the Greek system would be based on your personal merits, but that isn't always so.** For example, if you are a legacy (your parent or sibling was in the same house), you have a higher chance of getting into that house. Some houses choose based solely on GPA. Some care a lot about money, social status, or athletic ability. **If you don't get into a sorority or fraternity, don't worry**. Even at schools where half the population is in the Greek system, there's still half that isn't. There's plenty to do in college and you and your social life will recover in no time.

Top Five...
Essentials for Testing Well

* Water, water everywhere — nothing is worse than trying to concentrate while being thirsty.
* Extra pens or pencils.
* Eating something beforehand.
* Tissue and chapstick — you know you're going to want them.
* Comfortable clothes — dress well, test well.

Studies Show You Can't Party All the Time

Despite what you may feel your first week in college, it is perfectly acceptable not to be the partying type. Even if you love to go out, there will, I promise, come a day when you say, "Not again. Let's do something different tonight." Perhaps it'll be because you're tired. Perhaps because you've run out of money. Perhaps because you're beginning to fail Psych 101. **No matter the reason, there's plenty of great stuff to do that revolves a little less around alcohol and/or partying.**

If you don't want to drink, just say so when the beer comes out. Get a can of soda or some water. Nobody really cares — drinking at college is way too easy to be considered as cool as it was in high school. If you really don't like parties, plan something else.

This isn't exactly an advice section, because you're not dumb, and you can think of things to do. But, since two heads are always better than one, I'll throw out a few of my own favorites.

* Weekly poker game
* Anything outdoors in the dark (preferably with snow)
* Kickball
* Board games (the more players involved, the better)
* Betting games ("I bet you can't eat this in under a minute")
* Video games
* Going to a play, coffee house, or concert
* Learn guitar (first project is to find a guitar)
* Work out
* Read
* Giant game of Capture the Flag
* Have a BBQ
* Karaoke (the more embarrassing the better)
* Bowling
* Truth or Dare

I could go on and on, but I'm tired so now it's your turn. Have fun.

Going to Campus Events

I'm just going to jump right into this: **go to campus events.** You'll go to what seems like three hundred *a capella* concerts your first week of school, see maybe one play, and then stop, claiming you are too busy, don't have the money, or have better things to do. All of these are weak excuses. I'm not suggesting you must go to every event that exists, but college is filled with the coolest opportunities and activities, and all you need to do is show a student ID or shell out a few bucks.

Every school, no matter the size, is covered (and I mean *covered*) with signs and posters advertising different bands, speakers, rallies, dance performances, etc., every single week. Even if you just go to one event every month, you're bound to see at least twelve great things. When else will you get to see that performance of Javanese fighting puppets or meet the ambassador from Norway? No matter what you like to do, there's going to be something going on any given weekend, or even weekday.

It's tempting to go only to shows that your friends are in. Try to avoid this habit. There is no reason to limit yourself. **Be on the lookout for great speakers**. Groups often get famous or smart or cool (or all three) people to come speak, but because of poor advertising or student apathy, very few people attend. Even if you've never heard of the person, chances are he or she has something interesting to say, or he or she wouldn't have been invited in the first place. If you're at all interested in writing, go see a couple of authors read their works, even if it's not your favorite genre or you don't know their writing. In a small setting, you can probably meet the speaker afterwards and get the opportunity to ask questions you normally would never be able to. Bottom line: campus events rock. Give them a chance and I swear that your college career will be better for it.

Now here's one last important campus activity that you can go to if you're ever bored, looking for a laugh, or in the school spirit mood: good old-fashioned sporting events. If you're really excited about this idea, skip to the next section. If you're currently groaning, let me explain to you why sporting events are great.

Here's the first scenario: your sports teams rule. The games are great because everyone cares, and with good reason. **Even if you're not into sports, nothing is more fun than cheering on a winning team. Buy a school shirt, get some friends, and head to a stadium and scream your lungs out.** If nothing else, it's a good study break.

On to the second scenario: your sports teams are terrible. And I mean really bad. Sometimes this is a lot more fun than having good teams. **Being an underdog means you don't take games quite as seriously.** With no race to the championships, everyone is free to have a little more fun. Paint your faces and run around. Make up crazy cheers. Do whatever you want (within reason: if for some reason you want to drive a forklift onto the basketball court during the game, don't).

Right now you may be thinking, I don't like baseball, football is confusing, and basketball isn't that great. Fine, but that doesn't mean you have to give up on sports altogether. Root for the lesser-known teams; they'll love you for it. My roommate plays volleyball and I get a huge kick out of going to our gym and seeing her. There aren't that many fans, but I've made friends in the stands and we have a great time. Watch your golf team tee off, watch the birdies fly at a badminton tournament, and cheer on your ultimate frisbee team. Go see some people (guys or girls) get mauled in a rugby game (seriously, "mauling" is part of the game). These sports are usually played for the love of the game, and can be great fun to watch. Whatever your sporting style is, give athletic events a chance. You're bound, at the very least, to be entertained.

Getting Off Campus

I recently asked a friend who attends college in Boston why she doesn't go out more in the city, taking advantage of all the stuff she could be doing. Her reply: "I work too much." Don't let this answer be yours. **School work is incredibly important, true, but so are your life and your sanity. There is so much beyond your dorm room or college quad, but you have to take the initiative to go find it.**

It's easy to be entertained exclusively on your university's campus. There's plenty to do, your friends are there, and there's always work to be done. But these attractions don't outweigh what you have to gain beyond the bounds of your school. Explore your surroundings, meet different people, find something new that you enjoy.

Don't get trapped in the bubble that is college. College is much more than old buildings and large lecture halls. It's about exploring the world around you, interacting with new things and people, and finding out where you fit. You can't do this in your dorm room, in class, or at the student center. Get in your car, a bus, or a train. Hey, walk if that's what you want. Just get out. Go to a tiny art gallery or a world-famous museum. See an unknown pianist play or a huge rock concert. If you're short on funds, read the papers and find a free event. Even a school in the middle of nowhere has some sort of town. Go explore it, volunteer, work, whatever. Getting off campus can be the best learning experience you have, and certainly one of the most important.

Beware the Computer

No "social" section of a book about college would be complete without the three things that can make you the most anti-social person on campus: an instant messaging service, a way to download music, and the most addictive computer game ever. I'll start by saying two things: (a) Modern technology is a great, great thing, and (b) There should be therapy groups to help people stop using it.

I'm willing to bet that you have instant messaging (IM), listen to downloaded music, and play computer games already. But nothing, *nothing* compares to what happens when your parents disappear and your high-speed Internet connection arrives.

IM is great. It's a free way to talk to people long distance. It allows you to make plans while others are on the phone and lets you tell the world funny quotations or stories you have. **But (and I'm lecturing myself here, too), be careful how much time you spend on your computer.** Instant messages can easily suck your days away and are an easy way to not finish papers, waste four years, and eliminate contact with real, living, breathing people. (Trust me: it took me six hours to write this page.) To be excessively dramatic, don't sell your soul to IM — remind yourself that you have a life outside of your computer.

Another time bandit is the constant urge to download new, old, terrible, or funny songs. Lots of people download music, and you might too. **As time goes on, there are more and more legal consequences to "stealing" music, so be careful.** And if you do spend time downloading music, make sure it's not too much time. You'd be surprised how many people actually miss classes because they find their hands suddenly surgically attached to the download button.

Next we have the wide world of Internet computer games. When you plug into your dorm room Ethernet jack, you'll find you have access to a new world of gamers. Some undergraduates play casually; some never get up from their chairs and never become graduates. If multi-player computer games have always been your thing, I suggest a happy medium. I know this advice isn't rocket science — I'm just advising that you think about this before you get to school. **Consider what you want to get out of college**

academically and socially. Don't isolate yourself from people for the sake of a game. If you're really into them, great. But try to join a gamers club (if there isn't one, start your own) and make your interest a way to meet new people with common interests. Don't be the guy who always has his door shut or keeps his roommates up late at night just so he can play backgammon against someone in Australia. Again, it's all about moderation.

Last, but certainly not least, is every college student's best friend and worst enemy: Snood. If you haven't heard of Snood, you soon will. It's a downloadable computer game of deadly, addictive simplicity. Okay, I'm exaggerating. There's nothing evil per se about the game, but for some reason it's almost impossible to resist playing for hours. **I've had over twenty friends actually delete the game from their systems because it was hurting them academically and socially**. I believe the creator now (wisely) charges for the game, so maybe fewer students play it. Snood is great fun, but I suggest you only play it on other people's computers. That way you can break their records and not worry about being tempted to play when that ten-page sociology paper is due.

Top Five...
Studying Pitfalls to Avoid

* Leaving the TV on all day, every day.
* Studying with your boyfriend/girlfriend.
* Leaving Instant Messenger on while studying.
* Thinking that planning to study counts as studying.
* Deciding that no sleep is better than a little sleep.

The Section Your Parents Don't Want You to Read

You guessed it, it's on to K-I-S-S-I-N-G — more specifically dating and sex in college. I can't say that you should or should not date in college. **Most schools have different dating cultures. Some are full of serial daters who never settle down; at others everybody either has lots of hook-ups or long-term serious relationships. Whatever the customs of your new home, you should be prepared.**

College is a bizarre time. You're on your own, living with your friends, thinking (I hope) independently. In short, you are an adult. But you're also eighteen, you probably rely on your parents for most of your worldly possessions, and you don't have a clue what you want out of life. In short, you are not an adult. It's difficult enough to navigate this thin line comfortably, let alone when it comes to dealing with another person. **Still, there is a way to survive the college dating scene: (1) Follow your head, not your body; (2) Follow your heart, not your head**. If you're alert, right now you may be thinking, "So you're saying that I should use my head, not my head?" Quiet, you, and listen to what I have to say.

Follow your head, not your body.

This is the "Be Smart" plan, the one your sex-ed teachers, your parents, and maybe even your older sister always preach. It's pretty self-explanatory. Even if you don't have a boyfriend/girlfriend or a crush, there will come a time when you will have urges to do things that perhaps aren't, let's say, wise. Try to take a step back from your urges and say, "Wait, s/he's been with six of my friends already," or "Hey, my boyfriend/girlfriend isn't going to like hearing about this." **Don't put yourself or your relationship in danger either emotionally or physically for a few moments of gratification. It's just not worth it.** I'm sure your high school teachers showed you enough gross pictures of strange diseases that I don't need to tell you why being careful is essential. Nevertheless, your health center has a private, confidential, and (despite popular belief) fairly competent sexual health department that can help you out with any "problems" you may have. Basically, think before you act, not ten minutes after. And if you do something stupid, go to the health center ASAP, not next week or next month.

Follow your heart, not your head.

Welcome to the second half of my contradictory advice. Having just told you to think, let me tell you not to overthink. College is one of the last times you have when you can date someone with whom you have no future or date several people simultaneously, both without having to worry. So don't worry. Live a little. Who cares if you go out with someone who is your total and complete opposite? You're not looking to get married just now, and who knows, maybe you're actually perfect for each other. Don't get wrapped up in mind games. **If your friends don't think your new guy is cool, ignore them. If your parents say that your new girlfriend isn't ambitious enough, say that's fine and continue to do what you feel. The heart is smarter than most people give it credit for and, while it might mess up, this is exactly the time to risk letting it do so.**

After the thinking and the not thinking, we come to... sexual etiquette. Not what you do or don't do in private, but how your love life plays in the rest of your world. **There are two huge problems that college students commonly face — trying to get rid of your roommate for the night and what to do when you get kicked out of your own room.** This is commonly known as "sexiling." It's easy to ask your roommate to leave every time you have your boyfriend or girlfriend over. But before you jump into this plan, try to remember what will happen when your roommate gets a significant other. Let me break it up into simple sentences: You. Sleeping. Outside. On the floor. Sound good? I thought not. No one likes to be kicked out of his or her own bed, especially over some new person. It's unreasonable to believe that this situation will never arise, but try to keep it to a minimum. Maybe work out a deal with your roommate or significant other where you will alternate rooms if you want to be alone.

On the other side, don't be scared to stand up for yourself. You paid for your college dorm room and it is yours to sleep in. You have no obligation (other than politeness) to leave your bed for the sake of your roommate's privacy. If you feel the situation is getting out of hand, talk to him or her. If that doesn't work, either put your foot down or talk to your RA.

If you are bringing someone home on a regular basis, try to make it easy on your roommate. Try to hang out with both of them at once so that they are comfortable around each other. Make sure there is a mutual respect and understanding. **Most importantly, make sure your date never ever hogs the bathroom and never ever leaves tons of stuff in your room.** This is a cardinal rule of happy roommate relations. If you have a shared hallway bathroom, this shouldn't be an issue. But if you share a bathroom within a suite, realize that while you care for your girlfriend or boyfriend, your roommates care for their bathroom. Don't let your significant other stand in there for hours getting ready and don't get frisky in the shower.

Also, even if your boyfriend or girlfriend stays in your room every night, do not under any circumstances say, "Hey, why don't you leave your books here, and your clothes, and your everything." It's not his or her room, no matter how comfortable your roommate may be with him or her. **Realize that even if your roommate doesn't say anything, he or she is probably just being polite. Dorm rooms are small. Don't add another person.** This is not to say that having another person over at night can't be fun. My freshman year I knew two roommates who both had their boyfriends sleep over every night. But this is, to say the least, not for everyone.

Remember to keep relationships in perspective. If you find yourself in a semi-serious relationship freshman year, (1) yay, and (2) be careful. No, I'm not talking about being "safe," I'm talking about making and/ or saving your other friendships. Freshman year is like no other time in your life in terms of the number of people you'll meet, and it's important to have a group of friends that you can turn to when things get tough and you need to de-stress.

Do not, under any circumstances, let your relationship keep you from making as many friends as possible.

Finally, remember to keep relationships in perspective. Everyone believes that his or her romance is the one that will last, that they're the freshman year sweethearts who will be together at graduation. Um, probably not. If you close yourself off, hanging out with only your "true love" freshman year, you could easily find yourself single and without many close friends come the following September.

Give yourself some space. Don't live in each other's rooms. Make friends independent of each other, and don't be that gooey-eyed, all-over-each-other couple that no one wants to be around. Chances are your friends will be around longer than your significant other, and these are the people you are going to want to turn to should things go wrong. Make sure you actually have friends you can turn to. Besides, giving yourself space makes the time you do spend with your boyfriend/girlfriend that much better.

All of this applies to long-distance relationships that continue after high school. While you obviously won't be living in each other's rooms, you could attach yourself to the phone. Don't do it. Live your own life and let the relationship happen naturally. It's tough, but having made the choice to go to separate schools, you each need to be full participants at your schools. Don't isolate yourself or you will end up being lonely and unhappy where you are. Be where your body is. It is entirely possible to commit yourself fully to your relationship and to your school. Besides, what's the fun of a visiting significant other if you have no friends to show him or her off to?

Finally, I can boil all relationship advice down to one thing:

RESPECT.

There, did I write it big enough? I hope so. Respect others and you shall be respected. Or at least you'll have a better chance of it.

"WILL THIS BE ON THE TEST?"

Surviving and Thriving in College Academics

Picking Your Classes

Picking classes is one of the few really important things you have to do before you even step onto campus for the first time. **I'm not sure why, but schools seem to feel that some time between the last day of high school and the first day of college you gain a complete understanding of where you want your life to go and can thus choose classes wisely.** Not to have a lack of faith in you or anything, but I highly doubt this is true.

After you admit to yourself, your mom, and your dog that you don't really know what kind of classes you want to take or should be taking, sit down and read your course catalog. **Colleges have more classes, and certainly more kinds of classes, than high schoolers ever knew existed.** Suddenly you go from having to pick between "English" and "English Honors" to choosing between "Ideas of Pacifism in Seventeenth-Century British Literature" and "Lyric Poetry Between the World Wars." It makes perfect sense that you won't even know where to start. Well, here's where:

(1) **Read the entire course catalogue.** Come on, it's not that long. Well, maybe it is. But surely you're interested in the classes your new school has to offer. I promise it won't take that long. Skim through and circle anything and everything that slightly catches your eye.

(2) **Read the course catalogue again.** This time do it with a more discerning eye. Sure, a film class sounds cool, but do you really want to spend an entire semester breaking apart the films you love? Would you rather be investigating what makes clouds or even taking a screenwriting class? Think realistically about what kinds of classes you would enjoy studying, and even what format you would best thrive in (a twelve-person seminar or a large lecture class).

(3) **Get reading.** Most schools have some sort of online or paper version of a rating system of its classes. These feature the results of old class surveys and/or actual reviews written by students, and can be your best source of information. Don't get lazy — find them. **Only people who have taken the classes will be able to tell you that a professor is brilliant but a bad lecturer, or that you should try to get into**

a certain lab section. Still, don't blindly listen to the reviews you read. **Recognize that you don't know the people writing and that they probably have different academic styles.** If the reviewer writes that a class is bad because the lecturer never shows up, that's one thing, but if she writes, "This class is stupid because there's lots of reading," this person doesn't like doing work. You may be looking for a challenge and love the class.

(4) **Check the reputation of the professor**. Once you've found a group of interesting classes that have received reasonable reviews, it's time to do the smart thinking. **It is a widely acknowledged rule that no matter the subject, if you have a great professor you will love the class you are taking.** Research your potential professors. Read books he or she has written. If you like what you find, take a risk on the class. If he or she sounds boring, skip the class, even if the topic sounds good. A class on an unfamiliar topic with a great professor will be worlds better than a class on something you think you know and like with a terrible one.

(5) **Try to talk to professors.** This may be scary because it involves actual contact not only with someone you don't know, but also someone who may be a bit intimidating. Still, this can be really helpful if you have any specific questions about a class. **So bite the bullet, give the professor a call, send an e-mail, or visit during office hours.**

(6) **Broaden your horizons.** Don't take the same types of classes you took in high school. You're going into a new place, take new classes, explore. **College isn't meant to be High School, Part II, so don't treat it that way. Choose wisely and choose creatively.**

Getting into Closed Courses

The dirty little secret of college catalogs is that you can't always take the classes listed. If you go to a medium-sized or large school, and especially your freshman year, you may find it extremely difficult to get into all the courses you want. It's not uncommon to find that you can't take classes your school actually *requires*. Before you pull your hair out at the insanity of this, or give up and take something in which you have no interest, let me give you a word of advice: *beg.* **Beg to get into classes. Be annoying.**

Well, not too annoying. Before you go poking your potential professors over and over until they turn around and listen to you, let me explain what I mean. **Just because a course is listed as closed, or "open to sophomores only," or "by permission of instructor," this does not mean you can't get in. Accepting "no" the first time is for amateurs.** If you really want to be in a course that is closed, there are several steps you can take.

First, **put your name on the waiting list**. Many people sign up for more classes than they can possibly take or ones they may not finally want so that they can pick and choose later. You could find out as early as the first day of class, sometimes sooner, if you're in. Putting your name on the list involves no more effort than writing your name.

Even if the waiting list doesn't open up before classes start, show up for the first day of class. Sit in the front. Take notes. Prove you care enough to come even though you might not be able to get credit. Now, you're primed for step three: asking the professor directly if you can be in the class. Don't spend a lot of time begging people in the registrar's office to allow your name to be added to the list. Your professor is sometimes the only one who can say "yes" to you definitively. Be respectful, but be persistent, and make it known that you really want to be in the course. Professors love when you're interested. Shocking, I know. Above all, be polite. You will need help from these people again, and believe me, it's for the best to be on everyone's good side.

Top Five...
Foods to Always Have in
Your Room

* M & Ms
* Apples
* Ramen noodles
* Peanut butter
* Bread, any kind

Fulfilling Requirements

Most schools have a set of classes all students have to take — distribution or "core" requirements that range from the fairly easy to the extremely complicated and time consuming. If you're lucky, your school falls into the first category. In all likelihood, it falls somewhere in between the two. **The best advice I can give is to follow your school's requirements style**.

If your school has an insane number of requirements, take them very seriously and try to do them all fairly quickly. **Don't blow off anything, or you may find yourself unable to graduate**. If your school has very few requirements, it probably wants you to explore everything on your own, rather than helping you pick out specific classes. This can be a double-edged sword, but if you know what you're interested in, take those courses and make sure you fulfill your few core classes along the way.

If your school, like most, has some, but not an astounding number of requirements, be careful but not too careful. **Don't spend your freshman year fulfilling every requirement**. You have four years. Explore, experiment, discover. Take one or two required classes, and let the rest be up to you. **Nothing burns out a student like lack of enthusiasm for classes**. Also, you'll probably be required to pick a major, usually by the end of your sophomore year. It'll be extremely difficult to do this if you spend your first semesters fulfilling requirements. How will you know what you're truly interested in if you don't try new things out or explore your chosen field in greater depth? You won't.

At the same time, requirements are not going to disappear. Be aware of what they are and try to make a schedule in your mind or even on paper of when you want to fulfill them. Don't postpone the worst requirements until your senior year. No one wants to do three lab classes second semester senior year, especially when he or she is an English major. Don't miss out on cool stuff because you have to fulfill requirements. Find out what you have to do and get it done.

Teaching Assistants

What a teaching assistant, or TA, does is pretty self-explanatory. He or she is (usually) a grad student who aids your professor in teaching, explaining, and grading. TAs often teach the smaller "sections" of large lecture classes. At these sections, usually held once a week, you go over material from class, get into more specifics, and discuss homework. It is often the case that your TA may be the person who actually grades your exams and papers.

For all these reasons, **choose your TA wisely. Be aware that these people may affect your grades and enjoyment of a class far more than your professor. Unlike lectures, section classes meet at several different times. Most people pick their section according to their time schedule. Pick yours according to the TA.** Personally, I try to get into the small section that the professor is teaching, if possible. That way I know that what I learn in section is always exactly what the professor wants to impart and what will be covered in midterms and finals. Still, I've had great experiences with grad student TAs, and every one is different.

Moral of the story? Choose carefully, if possible. Find out about each TA, which section he or she will be teaching, and whether or not he or she has ever taught before. That way, if you're choosing between two possible sections, you can choose the one with the better TA. A little effort can save you from a mind-numbingly painful class.

Get Your Butt in the Chair

College is a no-brainer, right? You get up, you go to class, you take notes, you pass. If you're thinking "duh" to this, good, move on. If you're thinking "Class every day? Please, get real," it's time to read this section and read it well.

Classes are not optional. True, no one is waking you up in the morning to go to them, no one is paying attention if you really are in that large lecture hall, and no one is ringing bells to regulate where and when you go to class.

You'll probably love college because finally you're in charge. With no one watching you, you're free to live your life your way, your style. You pick your classes, you pick what you eat, you pick your friends and what you do. But don't use this power foolishly. Don't make a habit of ditching classes. Once you don't go to one or two, you could fall down a slippery slope of never going to class. Believe me, it happens.

Even if you have a course with exams based solely on the books you read, not the lectures, it's important to go to class. Why? Because I said so. Okay, that's not really the reason. It's because **your classmates are smart. Your professor is smart. They have things to say that you have never even thought about. College isn't just about grades, it's about figuring things out and learning how to think**. Find out other people's opinions and it'll spark new ones of your own. Plus it'll give you plenty of new ideas for that pesky final paper.

"My sophomore year a friend of mine took Psych 101. The class was huge and he was taking the class Pass/Fail. He rarely went to class and when he did he usually slept. He studied for the midterm, but failed it because it was based on a lot of what was said in class. He studied for two weeks just for that one final in order not to fail. He passed, but I think it would've been less effort just to go to class."

— John, University of Maryland

How to Study

Every person has his or her own study style. It may be best for you to spread out everything and do it at a relaxed pace. It may be that if you do things at the last minute, you are forced to create quality. **I can't critique your way of studying because to each his own and you've obviously gotten this far. However, I can guarantee you that what you are currently doing is not enough**.

That's right, not enough. For most, college is a different ball game than high school. **In high school you can take eight classes and have three tests on any given day and magically survive. In college, one test can take you down for a week**. It's not that the papers are so much longer (though they usually are) or that the questions asked are tougher (though that often is the case). It's that you need to realize that you can't do it all.

College is the land of reading. Books, course packets, articles, lab instructions. Lots and lots of reading. **Despite the gung-ho spirit you may feel going in, it is impossible to read everything you will be asked to read. Even more so, it's silly and counterproductive to try.**

In college, it's not about who studies the hardest, it's about who studies the wisest. Anyone can stay up until four AM every night trying to get every ounce of information out of a book, but that person isn't going to remember all that information, and could forget the one thing asked of him or her in class the next day.

Before you do any reading, look at the title of the book/article/ whatever and think about what you are learning in class. Then read intelligently. Read for the essential information and facts you will need to know the next day or for the final. If your class is in economics and the article is on family life in Botswana, concentrate on the section on farming and trade, not the part about marriage taboos. Knowing everything is great, but it won't get you as far as knowing the right things.

Taking Advantage of Resources

One of the reasons you chose your new school is its resources. **Your college will have more books, larger buildings, and better facilities than your high school**. People often brag about how their school's library is larger than any other in the world or that it houses an original manuscript by a famous author. Others boast the most advanced computer systems in the United States or even just wireless Internet all over campus. Yet others claim the best university pool in the nation, one used for Olympic trials. Even a tiny college is full of great stuff, whether it's a complete collection of missionary diaries or the world's only lab devoted to the study of a certain insect.

All of this is fine and good, but not if you don't take full advantage of all your school has to offer. I can't even count the number of people I know who have never been inside their university library. Most of these people even take great pride in this fact, as if making it through college without using the opportunities thrown at you is a badge of honor.

Get that idea out of your head now, because a school's resources are only as good as your use of them. Take the library tour, look through the university telescope, use your computer outdoors, go to the Saturday morning open swim. Even if you aren't studying ancient manuscripts, go to the library and ask to see them.

Often your school has much more to offer than it advertises. Most schools house collections of many rare things that only come out if someone asks. As a student, you are almost always allowed to look at your school's great stuff. For all you know, your library houses old film archives and your physics department has some rare scientific instrument.

You never know what you'll love and appreciate until you go and check it out. I know you love your couch (I certainly have a close relationship with mine), your friends, and your video games. But college passes, while friends and even couches endure. Get up and get a collegiate life.

Top Five...
Movies Every College Student Should See

* *Revenge of the Nerds*
* *Dead Poets Society*
* *Animal House*
* *With Honors*
* *The Princess Bride*

Office Hours

Bad grades happen, especially in college, and often in your freshman year. These bad grades can appear in your life for a variety of reasons: the material is new, the class is harder than any you've had before, you forgot to look up a definition or a supplementary reading, you were not destined to be a doctor or engineer after all, or more simply, you didn't study enough (or at all, in some cases — tsk tsk). Whatever the reason, a few bad grades are no reason to curse your professor and skulk into a corner, swearing never to take geology again or claiming that you are stupid. This is, in fact, the perfect time to pick yourself up, dust off that cramp in your GPA, and talk to your professor or teaching assistant. "What?" you say, "Go in there and draw more attention to the fact that I watched reruns of *The Sopranos* rather than looking up all the buildings in southern France that have Islamic arches?" Well, yes.

Professors are not evil. They are not paid to bring you pain, no matter how much they may seem to enjoy doing so. They decided to never leave school because they like it, and they like the idea of helping others like it as much as they do. Time and again, I have heard professors lament that they announce their office hours, only to sit there with their door open waiting for the seat opposite them to fill, almost always disappointed. Even if your professor does not hold office hours, chances are his or her TA does, and there is no reason not to employ this resource.

"I took an astrophysics class once in which I was completely confused, yet never did anything more than complain. Finally, at the end of the course, after our TAs practically begged us to come see them if we had issues, I went in and asked for some help with the homework. For the next hour, I had a TA going over every problem step by step. Sixty minutes later, not only did I understand what I was doing, my homework was done."

— Lauren, Florida State University

Dropping in during office hours has two uses. First, it can help you improve your grades. In humanities classes, it is often valuable to ask professors specific questions about why an essay answer did not receive full credit or a paper was deemed less than perfect, as you can learn your professor's grading criteria and not make the same mistakes on your next paper. **Don't expect an office visit to improve your past grade, however. Nothing ruins a good relationship faster than telling your professor or TA that you deserve or want or "need" a higher grade.** If desperate, ask about doing additional work to redeem past failures.

A second reason for frequenting office hours is to remind professors that you exist. Yes, even C-student, only-shows-up-for-half-the-classes you. Your appearance at office hours shows professors that you care, at least a little, not just about your grades, but about learning about the subject in which they have spent their lives researching and teaching. Even if your grades are fine, come to office hours! These people can give you advice in developing your interests, but they can't advise if you don't ask.

Most students I know cite two reasons for not going to office hours — they don't know when and where they are, and they are scared. Oh puh-leeeze, I say. Almost all professors or TAs have office hours. If you can't find the listing online, ask. I promise professors won't bite. I should know, since my dad is one. As children, my brother and I used to take great joy in answering telephone calls from frightened college students asking in a wavering voice for our dad, "Professor Smith." We would cackle in glee at their fear, run downstairs to where our father was making our lunches for school the next day, and tell him he had a call. If you are ever scared of a professor, don't imagine him or her in underwear; just picture him or her putting chocolate graham crackers in a lunch bag with a peanut butter and jelly sandwich or teaching a toddler how to use Kleenex. Believe me, it works every time.

Asking for Recommendations

Ah, the age-old art of begging for a good recommendation. It's helped many a high school student get into college. You would think we'd have this down by now, right? Not so. But it's a sad fact that applications for summer jobs begin as early as first semester freshman year, so read carefully. **Asking for a recommendation is a delicate process. You need to find the right person, ask at the right time, and do so in the right way.**

This may be counterintuitive, but it's not always right to ask the person in whose class you have done the best. Getting an "A" in a large lecture course does not mean that the professor can speak well of how you would do in the workplace. Your resulting recommendation would be vague and generic. A letter that states "Jimmy works well and has good attendance" is nothing compared to "Jimmy is a competent student who shows extensive personal interest and knowledge in the subject. He is an outstanding speaker and works well in small and large groups."

It is much, much, much better to ask someone who knows you well, a professor you worked with closely or somehow got to know beyond the "Will this be on the test?" conversations. Some of my best recommendations have come from professors who have given me less-than-stellar grades, but who knew how hard I worked. I know it isn't that logical, but sometimes getting a recommendation from a class in which you did less than the very best work can help you a lot. Usually a job or internship interviewer asks for a copy of your grades. Your academic triumphs speak for themselves. Your "bloopers" may need an explanation.

While it is always a good idea to try to get a recommendation from someone who both knows you well and gave you a high grade, getting a glowing recommendation of your effort and dedication, regardless of the grade, can show someone that while you were not a natural star in the class, you have the strength of character to see something challenging through. Of course this doesn't work if your grades were your own fault; a bad grade and an only so-so recommendation do nothing together but make you look like a mediocre candidate. A professor who thought highly of your work and knows you well is always the first choice for a recommendation.

Try to think ahead. Even if you aren't thinking about it now, you will need a recommendation at some point in your college career, be it for a job, internship, or grant. Do your best to get to know at least one professor (preferably two). Go to office hours, show up for review sessions, ask questions. When it comes time the professor will remember and be able to write about you.

If you are lucky enough to find a professor early on who shows an interest in your academic career, keep in touch after the class is over. I'm not saying have long lunches, but an e-mail or two per year saying how something reminded you of his or her class or offering an update on something you once talked about will make it less awkward to ask for a recommendation later on. Besides, these people can give great advice, have interesting opinions, and be fun to talk to. Really.

If you have more than one professor from whom it would be possible to ask for a recommendation, think out who would truly be the best person to ask. I've had lots of great teachers, but maybe my geology professor wouldn't be the best person to ask for a job at a fashion house. Your recommender doesn't have to be a perfect match — it makes sense that a math teacher could discuss your ability to work in problem-solving groups at an advertising agency — but consider which skills your future employer might want and try to find someone who could speak well of you and those skills.

Once you've zoned in on someone you would like to write a recommendation, consider your timing when you ask. **Professors and administrators are busy people.** They write a ton of recommendations every year, as well as teach, grade papers, research, and spend time with their families. **Find out when your recommendation is due and what type of information is needed. Give your writer at least a month, if possible, to write your recommendation, especially if he or she is fairly young and may not have written a lot of recommendations before.** Giving plenty of warning is a sign of respect and that you have thought things through carefully, and this will result in a better letter for you.

I usually e-mail my recommendation requests and follow up if I don't hear back within a week. **Thank the person in advance and state that you know that writing for you may not be possible.** Also, most writers ask for a resume and list of classes from you, so have those ready. **If you think there is a chance that the person could say no, however, I suggest going to see him or her in his or her office. This is sneaky, but it's always harder to say no to someone who is standing in front of you.**

If a professor does say no due to time issues or the fact that he or she wouldn't have enough to say about you, be polite. Say thank you for his or her consideration and look for someone new. **If the professor says yes, be extremely gracious. Remember that your professor is taking time to do something completely selfless — it's not exactly a party writing all these recommendations**. Get your materials to the recommender on time. Include a stamped addressed envelope to its final destination. Thank the person at the time and later when the recommendation is sent. Also, let the person know how your application turned out, if you got the job, and, later, how it worked out, including if you had the internship from hell. Professors appreciate politeness and they care about results. Since this is one of the few ways in which college resembles the real world, treating your professors the same way you should treat your future boss is excellent practice in becoming a full-grown functioning adult.

Politeness serves beyond just getting a recommendation. A friend of mine thanked her lab professor profusely for a job recommendation and then wrote him a few times over the summer about how much she loved her job. The next summer he let her know about a similar job he had heard about and wrote her another glowing recommendation. She was way ahead of the competition because of her polite and thoughtful e-mails.

Organizing Your Time

Let me introduce you to a good friend of mine, someone who will help you enjoy college to its fullest, getting everything done without any unnecessary stress. My friend's name is Organization. Yes, that was corny, but seriously, if you get organized now you're going to be really, really happy with yourself later.

Without becoming a control freak, you can do simple, small things that will make your days freer and more fun, even when finals time seems way off in the future. **The best way to manage your time is to write down all the things you need to do.** Writing everything down helps you see how much, or how little, you have to do. You can gauge whether you should be starting your work early or worrying less. Prioritize what you have to do and chug through it all. Line it up, knock it down. Everything is more manageable when it's in simple list form in front of you.

Time management becomes especially tricky when you throw in an extracurricular activity or a job. As high school probably taught you, when you have class during the day and a job or sport after classes, you usually don't get around to work until well into the night. The best I can tell you is to realize that having a job or extracurricular activities involves sacrifices in other parts of your social life. **If you don't want all your free hours to be filled with work, try to wake up a little earlier and get work done when others are asleep, or bring your schoolwork to your job and try to get things done in your free time.** If you put everything off until tomorrow, tomorrow will be a terrible, terrible day.

Dealing with Success, Dealing with Failure

I highly doubt that every grade you receive in college will be fantastic or terrible. Thus, it's important to know how to deal with a full range of results. You know how to be average. Let's just deal with the extremes...

You ace a tough final, you're named captain of the basketball team, and you win three awards in one day. Success is a bit easier to deal with than failure. This is kind of obvious, but make sure you do it graciously. No one likes a bad winner. There, I said it: now make sure you remember it.

You receive an F, get rejected from the varsity team, and don't get the fellowship you applied for. Well, today hasn't been your best day, has it? Believe me, it's not as bad as it seems. I honestly believe that everyone needs an F at some point in his or her life. Do not give up. An F means you didn't study hard enough or study the right things, or maybe just don't have aptitude in a particular area — not that you are unintelligent. Don't get caught up and let one bad grade be a slippery slope of giving up on all your classes.

Here's a good motto to remember if you ever get down: **Even "D"s get degrees**. One bad grade doesn't dictate who you are or where you'll go in life. Of course, a string of bad grades can keep you off a team or take away your scholarship. Still, take it in stride and you'll have a better college career, as well as life.

As to sports, college teams are competitive. Join an intramural team if you really love to play. You'll have to devote less practice time than on a varsity or JV team and get more play time. Plus, you'll stress less and just enjoy the game.

If a grant proposal you make is rejected, pout a little and move on. My personal motto is that if you don't enter the competition, you can't win, but this requires applying for tons and tons of things. There's no way you'll get everything, so appreciate what you have and realize that sometimes there are better suited (or maybe just luckier) people.

My Memory Isn't What It Used to Be

Remember applying to college? It involved way too many essays, a lot of instances when you needed to write down your social security number, and possibly some begging for great recommendations. But you probably recall all that fun way too clearly. Here's a tougher question — do you remember **everything** you did in high school? Come on, wasn't it just recently that you were there? What do you mean you might have been in the Recycling Club freshman year? You don't remember your boss's name from that internship you had over winter break sophomore year? Come on now, what's going on?

I'll tell you what's going on — it's impossible to remember all the stuff you've done in the past, and it'll continue to be hard in the future. I don't care how great the experience was, how cool the co-workers were. Chances are you won't be able to recollect everything when it comes application time again, this time for internships, grants, and jobs with even larger stakes.

Serving on the dining hall improvement team could get you into culinary school, but not if you've forgotten about it altogether. Be smart and take twenty seconds to write down your supervisor's name and phone number and your activities as you join. If you quit, or don't really do much in them, the worst that happens is you cross them off your list. Believe me, it beats going through phone books trying to remember your boss's last name. Not that I've ever had to do that.

Top Five...
Reasons There's No Place
Like Home

* Free food.
* Parents dote much more when you're gone most of the year.
* There's nothing like your own bed.
* No need for an ID card to get into places.
* Free food (it's important enough to say twice).

A Word to the Unwise

Let there be no mistake: it is stupid to cheat on an exam or plagiarize a paper. Lest you think that I am kidding or that there is a way to get away with academic dishonesty, let me say it again and in bold: **you are stupid if you cheat or plagiarize.** There, I said it; I hope it wasn't too mean.

There are many reasons students cheat, but the point is not the reasons. The point is that no reason for cheating is acceptable. It doesn't matter if you're just lazy or your entire family suffered a horrible accident one week earlier. Whatever the reason, your school pretty much requires that you get punished for plagiarism or cheating.

Now you may think that the worst thing that can happen to you in college is failing. You may think it's not acceptable to come home with bad grades because someone is paying a lot for you to go to school. **Well, it's much less acceptable for you to get asked to leave school altogether. This is usually the punishment for any kind of cheating.** I can't stress this enough. There is no exception to the rule. You will be asked to leave school, or at least fail the class, and the incident will probably be put on your permanent record. Think three hundred times before you download a paper from the Internet or start to write the answers on the back of your hand.

Getting caught cheating is easier than you think. A lot of schools operate on the honor system. This is not an easy chance to cheat. Most exams are graded on a curve, and if someone in the class sees you cheating, they're probably going to think, "I studied all night just so he could get a better score than me?" **Turning in a cheater is anonymous and easy.** As for papers, there are programs designed to catch plagiarism. Professors can scan papers and the program will check the Internet for similar or identical ones. Also, don't underestimate a professor's memory. Students seem to think that they can take a friend's paper from the year before, change the title and the first paragraph, and call it a day. Professors are on the lookout for plagiarism. They will catch you. Cheating is a foolish game to play.

SOME STUFF FOR THE FOLKS AT HOME

Mom, Dad — Read This!

Surviving Life with your Pre-Frosh

So your son or daughter got into college. Good job, you've passed step one of raising an independent adult. Now comes step two, that lovely three- or four-month period before college begins.

I'll be blunt; **pre-frosh are hard to live with before they leave for school.** Expect some stomping, expect some yelling, and expect some fights. Suddenly all your accepted rules are out the window and random moodiness reigns supreme. Don't worry, it won't last forever. This is normal and just an expression of your son or daughter's complete and total panic about going to college. Though your child may act cool, somewhere inside there is the person who cried the first day of sleepover camp and is worried about going to a new place, making new friends, and leaving home (and you).

The best advice I can give you is **don't fall for the act**. You love your child (or you wouldn't be reading this section), your child loves you (honest), and once the adjustment period is over, peace will return to your family. **Every time your child acts up a bit, shrug your shoulders, smile and nod, and move on**. College is scary, but doable. Understand the fear, but don't give in to it. And if it gets really bad, just remember soon you get to send him or her away for months on end, and it'll only cost you thousands of dollars. Per year. For four years. At least.

Yes, I Really Do Need This Shirt!

Packing is one of the great joys of college. And by joys, I mean pains. **Your child will insist on bringing way too much clothing to school, and it is pointless to argue**. The only response that will be accepted is help choosing one of three identical T-shirts. When you're a freshman worried about making a good first impression, it's hard not to insist that at some point you really will need two pairs of Hawaiian shorts and every pair of shoes you own. As soon as your child moves in and realizes real dorms rooms aren't the size they are on TV, half the clothes will be coming home at winter break. Just try not to say, "I told you so."

Moving in, Moving on

Before I get to the emotional part of move-in day, I'm going to let you in on a mystery of college life. **Unless your child is going to the University of Alaska (and possibly even then), move-in day will undoubtedly be the hottest day you have ever experienced**. Wear shorts. Wear an old T-shirt. Wear steel-toed boots. **If at all possible, find young, fit college students milling around the dorm and ask them to help move your child's things into his or her fifth-floor room**. There is nothing, *nothing* better than having the luxury of embarrassing your child slightly and saving your back completely by asking strangers for help. I guarantee it's well worth the soft drink or even the five bucks you may give them at the end.

Now that the logistical issues are out of the way, be aware that move-in day will also be filled with tension. **The second their belongings enter their dorm, freshmen freak out**. They want to disavow everything associated with their old life, starting, of course, with you. You will be embarrassing, you will be annoying, you will be asked to leave immediately or (if still unpacking) to never speak or at least to become invisible. **Just as you did while living with your pre-frosh, on move-in day the best you can do is tolerate the verbal abuse.** Agree to everything (except handing over the credit card), take nothing personally, and move-in will be as smooth as possible.

Even if he or she was angry ten minutes earlier, when it comes time for you to leave, don't be surprised if your child gets upset. You'll probably be experiencing the same tidal waves of sadness, excitement, and nervousness. Whether your child seems indifferent or is crying as you leave, your approach should be the same. Smile, give your son or daughter a big hug, ten bucks for dinner that night, and say goodbye. **Whatever you do, don't linger. Staying around too long is counterproductive (your child has a ton of new people to meet) and only prolongs the separation anxiety**. Yank the Band-Aid off and leave. **When it's time to go, go**.

Pick up the Phone

The first few weeks of school are tumultuous for new college students. They meet five hundred new people a day, navigate a wide array of distant and poorly labeled buildings, and generally learn how to live on their own. It's likely you'll get a bunch of calls during this time (or none at all, but that's usually not a bad sign). Console your child, say he or she made the right decision, encourage him or her to go out and do things. Freshman anxiety is normal.

Usually students start out a bit depressed or anxious at a new place, then rise quickly in spirits as they meet new people and see all the exciting things they can do. After a bit, the newness wears off and students may become depressed again. But usually they settle in and the new place becomes home. Things look up and level there. Don't dismiss his or her fears, but tell your child that things will almost certainly get better. While it's annoying, major life adjustments just take time.

After the first few months, however, take these phone calls a bit more seriously. **Listen, and listen well, to what your child is saying**. This does not mean panic. Calls or letters of despair could easily just be signs of loneliness, boredom, or simply missing you. Don't immediately buy a plane ticket and jet over to campus. Don't cry that you are a bad parent who has sent your child off to the wolves. Chances are the mood will pass before long.

Call back a few hours later. If things still seem really grim and you're worried, **suggest that your child go talk to a friend, the RA, an administrator, psychologist, or anyone else who spoke to you on move-in day about issues just like these.** These people have seen countless freshmen come and go, and they can make recommendations based on that experience. At most schools the first few sessions with a psychologist or psychiatrist are free. Encourage your child to try out the health service. Finally, relax. I know it's hard, but don't worry too much. Odds are your child will be okay. The worst that happens is that he or she comes home and you all start anew, more aware and experienced.

Top Five...
Signs You've Lowered Your Standards Since Entering College

* Mail is the single most exciting thing that has ever happened to you.
* You find yourself stuffing day-old muffins in your shirt to take home from the dining hall.
* Suddenly wearing pajamas to class is A-okay.
* Courses that meet in the auditoriums with nice chairs excite you.
* You are willing to marry the person who moved your clothes into the dryer for you.

Home Sweet Never Home

When your child leaves for school, a constant stream of collect calls may make you believe that you are the only person your child wants to see when he or she first comes home. Well, brace yourself. **You will pick your child up at the airport or train or bus station, there will be hugs all around, maybe a meal, and then you will not see him or her until roughly around the time you drive him or her back to the station.**

As with every great breakup, it's not you, it's me (well, your child). Your son or daughter will want to see his or her high school friends. These are the people to whom freshmen feel closest. They have plenty of new friends and events to talk about, but are eager to share it all with their high school buddies. **Accept that you won't see your child very often, be happy he or she has such good friends, and try to make a few dates to hang out.** Throwing in a free movie or dinner never hurts at the bargaining table, and neither does offering food to the entire high school gang. Try to be around when your son or daughter wakes up. You can snag a few morning (or afternoon, as the case may be) minutes together before he or she whizzes off to someone else's house.

Sealed with a Kiss

Here is the surest way to get calls, hugs, and gratitude from your child away at school: send packages. I don't care if it's keys to a new car, cookies, or a random article you clipped from the newspaper. Students looooove to get packages. Mail is extremely exciting, especially if it's not junk mail or a bill. Packages are especially important around exam time. Fill a box with random things that can be tasty and distracting. Send hard candy, packets of microwave popcorn, an interesting pen, and a fun small toy or game. Though it would have seemed stupid to me in a store, I had a great time freshman year playing with my roommate's electronic noise-making yoyo when it came time to write my third twenty-page paper. Never underestimate the stuff you find lying around in your house. No package is too small.

SO, TO SUM UP...

So you've read the book. Or maybe you're one of those sneaky people that skips to the end first. Either way, as you know or are about to find out, college is crazy. It'll suck away your time, make you cry, give you friends you'll have forever, and prepare you to do what you swore you never would: get a real life.

What else is there for me to tell you, now that you know it all? Enjoy your friends, tolerate your relatives, drink plenty of water, and rest assured that ten years from now both your mistakes and your certainties will seem really, really funny.

THE NAME GAME

A Quick Guide to College Titles

Every school has its own special names for things. Here are a few of the most common.

Administration/Administrator — A person who manages or supervises a certain aspect of the school. Although they do no teaching, these people often control your life, standing between you and your ability to bend official rules (for example, turning in a final paper late).

Adjunct professor — A professor who has been added to university staff only temporarily. No tenure, no status, but often a great teacher. Often has another career (i.e., painter, lawyer, journalist).

Assistant professor — Usually someone in their first seven years of college teaching. Often just out of graduate school, not yet tenured.

Associate professor — The next rank above assistant professor. Usually has tenure.

Athletic director — The person who oversees all athletic teams and events. A huge power at big schools with large sports budgets. He or she is usually in charge of such things as scheduling intramural games and making sure that sports events run smoothly.

Bursar — The person in charge of university funds; similar to a treasurer.

Bursary — The place you go to cash checks, pay school bills, and pick up paychecks from campus jobs.

Chair — The faculty member in charge of a particular academic department (for example the chair of the chemistry department).

Chaplain — A person (usually a clergyman) who conducts religious programs and exercises.

Dean — General name for the highest administrator in a certain area. All colleges and universities have many deans.

Dean of Freshman — The person in charge of handling first-year academic issues.

Development Office — Development is a code word for raising money. This office handles small donations and major gifts, as well as large fundraisers for the endowment.

Endowment — Think of it as your school's inheritance. Many schools live (or die) on the income from their endowments.

Faculty — The teaching staff of your school.

Infirmary — Where you go when you're sick or hurt or need any kind of medical help, from a flu shot to a session with a mental health counselor. Also known as the health center.

Information Technology (commonly known as IT) — Your new heroes. These are the people you call when you have issues with your computer.

Intercollegiate — Activities that occur between different colleges. This usually is used when talking about sports.

Intramural — Something conducted only within your school (literally, within the walls). These are the games you play against other teams at your school, rather than traveling to play other schools, as varsity sports do. They usually require less of a time commitment and can be a lot of fun.

Master — A person who officiates over a residential college (or a group of dorms). Masters are often like deans, but for a smaller group of students.

Post-doc — A person who is studying beyond a doctoral degree. Usually doing research in a science lab. May be a TA for a science class, but usually not on the faculty.

Provost — A high-ranking administrative officer in charge of the university faculty.

Quad — Short for quadrangle; usually a large open area in the center of campus surrounded by buildings. This is the pretty place on the front of all college catalogues.

Resident Advisor (RA) — Usually an older student who lives in the dorms with freshmen and is in charge of answering questions, holding study breaks, solving small problems, and preventing chaos.

Reading period — The time after classes end and before finals begin when you have time to write essays and study for exams. Every semester students try, and fail, to do an entire term's worth of work during this period.

Refectory — The dining hall. Don't ask me why they use the fancy word.

Teaching assistant (also known as a teaching fellow, graduate assistant, and endless other variations) — The person who generally teaches the smaller sections of large lecture courses, grades papers, answers questions, and does all the work the professor doesn't have time for.

Tenure — A lifetime teaching appointment. Very important to the faculty, important to you because tenured faculty are more advanced in their careers. They know the administrative ins and outs of your school and are good at advice and recommendations.

Visiting professor — A professor who is, uh, visiting, usually from another school for a semester or year-long period. Knows the subject, not the school.

Work-study — A program that allows students on financial aid to have campus jobs while attending school. Many scholarships are paid in part as work-study salary, and many work-study jobs on campus are only open to students on financial aid.

ACKNOWLEDGMENTS

I'd like to thank Dad and Jeremy, who are always there with good advice, some of which I even accept; the TEE for driving me everywhere; C-18 for convincing me I shouldn't repack my stuff and fly right back home; Karim who said it could be done; Seth and Rachel who have infinite patience; the Sexy Six for showing me the ropes; the Curly Girlies who taught me what being jejune is all about; and the Butler boys for moving in my stuff and giving me years of constant entertainment. More than anyone else, I'd like to thank my mother, who may not be able to spell but sure can edit.

ABOUT THE AUTHOR

Lucia Stella Smith (Princeton '04) grew up in the college town of Evanston, Illinois, as the daughter of two professors. Since graduating from high school she has laughed with eleven different roommates, mastered the fine art of dorm living, and studied such a wide variety of subjects that she has to consult her transcript to remember her courses. While in college she majored in art history, studied abroad in Italy, held several campus jobs, and participated in multiple extracurricular activities, from musical theater to intramural kickball. She wishes she had been given this book before she started college.